Recover: A Guided Journal to Healing

Written By: Kristen Webster

This book is dedicated to my sweet saving grace, Ariel Janelle Victoria. I needed to become the best version of myself for you. You are my sunshine, my motivation,, my heart in human form. I LOVE YOU more than you would ever know. I want to make sure that you understand love, and that love will understand you. Love will not hurt you, harm you, threaten you, or bring danger to you. Love is patient, it is kind, it does not envy, nor boast. Love you to life and for life.

Love,
Mommy

A guided journal for: Surviving emotional abuse, healing from a narcissist, an abuser, a yeller, underachievers with overarching ideas of self, and more. To help you become the best version of yourself and more. You SHALL #Recover!

DISCLAMER: I am NOT a medical doctor, therapist, counselor or psychologist. I am a woman that went through some shit that I NEVER thought I would experience. I have three degrees, which led me to the education field, and I loved a man that didn't make me his only choice. You will see some personal journal entries here that will guide you through your personal situation and help you write your thoughts out. You can start however you like. The first time I started healing, was the day I decided to choose myself again. What did that look like? What I thought it looked like was me getting my hair done, nails done, a vajacial (yep, a facial for your "girl"), exercising and eating my favorite foods.

What it really looked like was the day I served my now ex-husband divorce papers and my heart and head was in an all time knock out fight. You would not believe how many times I told my lawyer not to serve him the papers, because I wanted this to work. My recovery started in my tears, fears, anxiety and whirlwind of emotions and I decided to sit in those feelings, feel them, write about them, seek therapy and get to the root of these emotions.

That's the day that the little girl and grown woman started to heal simultaneously. Some things were rooted in me. Some things were unfamiliar to me. I didn't know that the things I had just experienced were abusive behavior. I grew up in church, so we were taught so many erroneous lies about keeping a husband. Honey, let me be the first to tell you that cooking, cleaning, having babies, sexing and anything that is seen as a "wifely duty" is a LIE and those are considered life skills. If you are a wife, it is a privilege that you get to do those things, not a RIGHT. I know that just made some people mad, but honey, EVERYTHING that I mentioned has a salary attached to it in the work industry. A person that wants to be kept, will be kept. It is about mutual respect, honesty and making sound decisions. Don't let anyone make you an option, you are the CHOICE. Relationship is deeper than just having love alone. If you are looking for the perfect partner, you will forever be alone. Although I am alone now, I am not lonely. Come on girl, let's get this journey started.

It is time to heal and recover. I hope you find yourself, your smile, your genuine joy again and love YOU.

With love,

Kristen

If you ever had the thought: I can't wait to heal from this emotional, mental and soul pain, YOU are NOT alone.

Dear Beautiful Girl, YOU started healing when YOU chose yourself again. #Recover

There is a LOT more to my story, but you would have to follow my YouTube channel: "Bees In My Coffee" to get more. Because frankly, bees should NOT be in your coffee, but it is a true story behind that title and revelation.

I hope this Journey Journal helps you as much it has helped me come out of one of the deepest, darkest places of my life.

Dear Heart:

I've been a bad protector of you. I let you out to play and sometimes that playing turned into paying. You've been punctured, wounded and abused. Not by other people, but by me as your carrier. I allowed other people to get into my head and I began to internalize everything they said. You've hurt because of loss and the feeling of being lost. I asked my creator for ways to heal you. Suggestions came from near and far. "Exercise" they said, "Eat right," "Go hang out," "Have Kids." I have done and tried these, and yet you still feel lonely sometimes. You've gotten to a place that you only want to be bothered when you WANT to be bothered and on your terms. I don't blame you. I do apologize and I will make a conscious effort to restore to you the joy we once felt together working in harmony. You are my favorite. You keep me alive, give me strength and push me to be better. Now we need the push for our music that's been sitting on you for years. I'm reconvening with you. I won't play Russian Roulette with you again.

~ Signed

Kristen, July 30, 2015

Date:

Your turn. Write a letter to your own heart:

Dear Heart:

Date:

When a woman loves harder than a man, she will most likely end up hurting more in the breakup. It is our nature to be nurturers. We will have a bleeding heart for a puppy with a minor cut. What we thought was a tragedy, was just an appearance of blood splatter. Heal your heart and set up perimeters~ Kristen

Journal your thoughts about your personal experience of overly loving someone:

Date:

Don't praise me in public and treat me like shit in private~ Kristen

Write a letter to yourself and talk about all the good. Let's go girl, we have things to do!!! Get to writing

Don't you DARE say you have NOTHING. You are freaking gorgeous, getting your life together and it is time to embrace this journey

Dear Beautiful Girl (Yep, I am talking to you, as you should talk to yourself. Now write):

Date:

I don't want to "feel healed," I want to BE HEALED before another relationship. I have to feel these feelings, and not try to suppress them. I am angry. I am sad. I am relieved. I am experiencing loneliness. I am experiencing loss. I am experiencing emptiness. April 25, 2020~ Kristen

Have you ever believed in someone so much that you sacrificed everything that you knew about yourself?   Girl ME FUCKING TOO.

Talk about that experience here and let that shit out:

Date:

He NEVER asked was I ok. August 25, 2019.

Now I look in the mirror and ask my damn self:

Do a mirror check: Look yourself in the mirror. What do you see? This can be an emotional experience, but let that shit out. Then come back here and write it out. It can be in long sentences, journaling sentences or bullet points. I just want you to #Recover #Heal and #Feel #WipeYourTears

Date:

Every time you let a person talk out of order to you, it opens doors for the generation (your kids, nieces, nephews, little cousins) under you to learn that behavior and think it is ok to accept it. STOP THAT. Get rid of those planted seeds, pluck them out by the root and #Recover

Journal about the time or times that you dealt with someone talking crazy to you. You know what I am talking about. The cursing, yelling, and it STILL triggers you to this day. They have moved on, and you still feel that sting: Yep, write that shit and get it out. Say whatever you want to say here. How you want to say it:

Date:

If you are fighting for a relationship, you must understand WHY you are fighting. Before you continue to threaten your future, revisit your past to understand how you arrived to the present. Too often we use scripture (if you grew up in church like I did) to redirect our total thinking and it allowed us to make erroneous decisions. It's ok to look back, revisit your pain and then move forward from there. You won't become a pillar of salt, but you will be "salty" that you did not recognize signs, and you are miserable in your life. Know where you are, but don't stay there. Go where you are appreciated and not tolerated. Sometimes that road will be you and only you, and that's ok.

Write about your childhood relationships that may possibly reflect your current(or not so current) love relationship. What are things that are familiar? What are feelings that are familiar? You may not remember the situation, but you remember how you felt and WHO made you feel this way (You will start a forgiving process of THAT person right now, so you don't have to revisit this again). THIS is pinpointing your pain and healing from the inside out:

Date:

I AM ENOUGH. I AM ENOUGH. I AM ENOUGH

Dear Beloved. Yes, you are enough. Now take this time to organize your thoughts

I am enough to_____

_____

_____

_____

_____

I am enough to_____

_____

_____

_____

_____

I am enough to_____

_____

_____

_____

_____

I am enough to_____

_____

_____

_____

_____

I am enough to_____

_____

_____

_____

_____

I am enough to_____

_____

_____

_____

_____

You are MORE than enough and don't let anyone tell you different.

Date:

I don't want to midwife anymore dreams.

I find myself in this shitty situation of a relationship and I want out. I don't want to midwife anymore dreams of OTHER people. January 28, 2018

This is a piece of my journal entry from the date listed. It was how I felt at that time and I stand on that same statement today. Do you find yourself pushing your significant other or those around you into their dreams and you totally ignore yours or forget them? Well Beloved, that stops today:

Write down your OWN dreams. Specify them. Be realistic. Make time for it. Break it down in parts. Dream girl, and go for it. Really. Go for it. WRITE IT DOWN HERE:

Date:

Don't allow anyone to be in control of your feelings: What emotion are you in control of today: Write it down right here:

Date:

Stop privately apologizing for public embarrassment~ Kristen

Have you ever been embarrassed by your significant other and you can relive that moment over and over again in your head, just like it happened yesterday. Yep, me too. You may NEVER get the apology you think you should get, but don't stay with a person who feels it is ok to do that kind of thing to you and you still crave them. WTF???? Who raised them? Anywho. WRITE THAT SHIT OUT RIGHT HERE and we are leaving it RIGHT HERE:

Date:

Keep your private life quiet~ Kristen

Write your own personal thoughts about anything you want here:

Date:

My mind and my body finally said, "AMEN" to each other~ January 25, 2017:

Amen simply means to agree. Your mind and body should be in a space that they always agree: Girl, what are you waiting for. Write some short term goals here. Meet them and come back to check this list off. If no one else agrees with you. You should agree with you. #Amen

Date:

Don't lose who you are in a relationship. Small things like making your password associated with them, symbols that remind you of that person can make you forget who you are. Simply because even with them being out of your presence, they are still walking in your mind. Don't get so caught up that you get let down. February 3, 2017~ Kristen

Who were you in love/like/infatuated with? Or you still are because this person is your spouse/ex-spouse/soon to be ex-spouse: Yep. Go delete that shit. Change your passwords. Pictures on your phone. LOVE ON YOURSELF GIRL! YOU ARE ALL YOU HAVE for the INTERNAL PARTS OF YOU....You know the drill.

Write:

Date:

I am cutting some relationships off because they are toxic, even those that I thought were close and I do love them, but I just can't do a continuous relationship with them.~ Kristen

Date:

I usually don't regret my actions, but there are a few that I totally want a do-over for~ Kristen

Do you have some regrets, but can't turn back the hands of time? Write about it here. What would your "do-over" look like. Write it down here, to get it out of your system and leave it here. We are moving forward:

Date:

Written words have always fascinated me, whether a song or diary entry. It embodies my soul and very being. Written words have become my therapy~ September 25, 2016~ Kristen

Date:

Order my steps that I may be guided, because when I take the lead I always get misguided. Help me!~ Kristen

Whatever your higher being may be (I believe in God, therapy and balance), Write a letter to your higher being and tell them the desires of your heart here:

Date:

Don't let anybody manipulate you by saying," Life is too short" when they have been harsh, dismissive, and disrespectful to your feelings. Life was too short when they did that shit, and yet they still did it. October 6, 2021~ Kristen

Write:

Date:

Guilt is what we do, shame is who we are. They can easily have a very thin line~ Kristen

Don't let anyone guilt trip you into anything. Don't blame, shame or guilt yourself into a depression. Write about a time you felt blame, shame or guilt. Let it out right here.

Date:

It is ok to reinvent yourself! Yep. Even at your age. If the pandemic taught us nothing else, it showed us that time waits for no one and we have access to a lot more things that can be done on an email, digitally and quickly~ Kristen

Write about what you can do to reinvent yourself (and possibly make some money on it). Go on girl! What are you waiting for?

Write:

Date:

Self-care is not always the SPA. Spa trips gives your outer appearance some love. Self-care is sitting in your feelings, feeling them and pinpointing the root that needs to be destroyed for you to live in your highest self and best version of yourself. Did you meditate today? ~ Kristen

Write:

Date:

Don't ignore the red flags girl! Don't override them trying to find the good. IT IS RED…

Write down some red flags! Ask yourself why you put up with them, and never put up with them again:

Date:

Don't feel guilty about letting go. Letting go and decluttering our soul makes it clear for what is to come and even if you do feel guilty~ October 5, 2021, Kristen

Date:

GIRLLLLL! TRUST your gut. There is a difference between a red flag and trigger. Don't let a gift giver override that feeling by love bombing you with things you like. NO MAM:

Write:

Date:

Sometimes you are not cutting people off, you are cutting off manipulation, disrespect, lies, mistrust and unfortunately that comes with the person being deleted from your life~ Kristen

Write:

Date:

Honey, you are not an option. If he/she doesn't want you and only you, allow him/her to leave. You are the only choice. Govern yourself accordingly, put on some mascara, a little lipstick, a cute outfit and go be great~ Kristen

Write:

Date:

Sweetheart, don't you DARE suffer in silence through emotional violence, physical violence, financial violence, mental violence or spiritual violence~ Kristen

Write:

My prayer is that you found some kind of relief from this journal. There will be more to follow. Until then, please visit my YouTube Channel: "Bees In My Coffee," because we all know that bees don't belong in coffee.

With Love,

Kristen

A very special thank you to Demita Woolfolk-Walton of Becoming Unbothered. You pushed me way beyond my limits and helped me without hesitation in this process. I love you to life.

Made in United States
Orlando, FL
05 January 2022

12921137R00037